STORY OF SCOTLAND'S Flag

Edited by Paul Harris

Saltire and Thistle Badge

Story of Scotland's Flag was published in 1992 by
Lang Syne Publishers Ltd.,
Clydeway Industrial Centre,
45 Finnieston Street, Glasgow G3 8JU.

and printed by
Dave Barr Print.

Origination by Eric Moore Studio.

Adapted by Paul Harris from
The Story of the Scottish Flag
by William McMillan and John A. Stewart
published in 1925 by Hugh Hopkins, Glasgow.

CROSS OF VICTORY

*T**he Saltire said it all. Wherever victory photographs were taken, Scottish soldiers were present, clear evidence of the role they had played in last week's daring armoured battles.*

So wrote the Defence Correspondent of 'Scotland on Sunday' at the end of the Gulf War in 1991. This was just one of the more recent examples of a long historical tradition of valour in the fluttering shadow of the Saltire: the flag of Scotland and the emblem of her patron saint, St. Andrew. St. Andrew is long supposed to have chosen to be crucified on a cross made up of two diagonal beams for he considered himself unworthy to suffer the same death as Christ on an upright cross. After his death, some of his remains are said to have been taken in the eighth century by St. Regulus, or Rule, to Kilrymont in Fife, afterwards known as St. Andrews, and, after a vision to King Angus, the white cross on a blue field became his everlasting emblem and an inspiration to generations of Scots.

Over the centuries, the Scots have placed his saltire on their flag and on the uniforms of their armies. In the bitter and bloody conflicts on the Scottish borders the great red upright cross of St. George and the diagonal white and blue of St. Andrew, markedly different in colour and form, so easily distinguished friend from foe.

3

VISION AT ATHELSTANEFORD

There is considerable evidence to show that flags were carried by the earliest Scottish kings. These were in the way of personal regalia rather than of national significance. The seals of early Scottish kings like Duncan, Alexander and David show them to be carrying a spear to which a small flag is attached. An account of the Battle of the Standard, written by St. Aelred, Abbot of Rievaulx Abbey in the north of Yorkshire in 1138, states that the royal flag of the Scots had upon it a dragon, but it is assumed that this was the flag of the king himself rather than of Scotland as a whole.

In earliest Scots history, St. Columba, the apostle of the northern Picts, was generally recognised as the patron saint of Scotland. With the departure of the Columban clergy, the veneration accorded to St. Columba was generally given up and St. Peter became the patron saint until a sudden conversion to his brother, Andrew, around the middle of the eighth century.

Popular legend – reported by several authoritative historians – has it that Saint Andrew appeared to King Hungus, or Angus, MacFergus on the eve of battle with the Saxons under Athelstane, near the village in East Lothian now known as Athelstaneford. Although that was as long ago as the eighth century – the year 736 being confidently asserted by some authorities – it is well chronicled in the 12th and 13th centuries. Spottiswood writes in the 'History of the Church of Scotland':

Hungus betook himself to prayer spending most of the night in that exercise. A little before day, falling into a slumber, it appeared to him that the Apostle of St. Andrew stood by him and assured him of victory, which vision, being related to the army, did much to encourage them. The history addeth that in the journey of the battle there appeared in the air a cross in the form of the letter X, which so terrified the enemies as presently they gave back, Athelstane himself being killed.

After the battle, Hungus – or Angus as he is better known – "did appoint the Cross of St. Andrew to be the badge and cognisance of the Picts, both in their wars and otherwise." Kilrymont, or Kinrimund as it was sometimes known, became known as St. Andrews and during the

Middle Ages became as important a place of international Christian pilgrimage as its better known counterpart, Canterbury.

In mediaeval times it was common for the banners of national saints to become regarded as the banners of nations and in this regard the widespread acceptance of St. Andrew, long before armorial bearings came into fashion, led in turn to the acceptance of the saltire as the national flag. By 1286, the Seal of the Guardians of Scotland already bears, on the obverse, the figure of St. Andrew on his cross.

Things were a good deal more complicated in England where several saints competed for a pre-eminent position: not only St. George was in the running but other hopefuls like St. Peter of York, St. Wilfrid of Ripon and St. John of Beverley were actively in the lists.

By the beginning of the 14th century, the St. Andrew's Cross was in common usage in both peace and war as a national emblem. At Longforgan, the tombstone of Sir John Galychtly and his lady – bearing the date 1400 – carries the figure of St. Andrew on his cross. In the summer of 1385, as the Scots made preparations to invade England, the Scots Parliament decreed inter alia that every man should wear the white cross before and behind.

Drawing by A. G. Law Samson

5

Saint Andrew ✤   Saint George ✤

Saint Edward ✤   Saint Edmund ✤

*"Item every man French and Scots [the Auld Alliance in practice]
shall have a sign before and behind, namely a white St. Andrew's Cross,
and if his jack is white or his coat white he shall bear the same white
cross in a piece of black cloth round or square."*

Blue as a background had not yet developed as the prevailing
colour and it has usually been assumed that this developed from the
azure blue of the celestial background of the battle vision. Some
sources, however, suggest that France was the source of this particular
inspiration. In the 15th century – when Charles VII was king – the
French flag consisted of a white upright cross on a blue background.
Other evidence – repeated by Sir Walter Scott suggests that the white
cross of St. Andrew was often used in silver colour but this should not
be taken as indicating any great underlying uncertainty about the
authenticity of the St. Andrew's Cross. Silver itself was, of course, in
common use for badges and the cross became the real badge of the
Scots. Also, in heraldic matters there was as yet little in the way of
regimentation or enforcement. Also, the availability of vegetable dyes
very often determined use of colours. In earlier times, for example, the
attainment of an azure blue was relatively difficult and a black
background was often used for the saltire.

The saltire, with its undoubted religious significance, was adopted
by Scotsmen who set off on the Crusades. It is recorded that Malcolm
de Lennox, his descendants the Earls of Lennox, and his followers set
off with flags and uniforms bearing "argent, a saltire engrailed between
four roses gules." Similarly, many noble Scottish families took up the
saltire as a part of the charge in their arms: the Bruces, Johnstons,
Kirkpatricks and, even, the Norman immigrants, Agnew of Lochnaw.
The Scottish branch of this family bore the saltire as part of its coat
since soon after its settlement in Scotland in the days of David II.

The increasing use of the saltire is demonstrated in the seals of
James I & II, as well as on the seal of the latter's wife, Mary of
Gueldres. A saltire appears on the seal of the Vicar-General and
Bishop's Official of St. Andrews in the fifteenth century and post-
Reformation seals of the dioceses of St. Andrews, Dunblane, Caithness
and Edinburgh all bear the St. Andrew's Cross clearly showing Roman

Earl of Lennox ❖ Lord of Annandale

Lord Maxwell ❖ Haig of Bemersyde

*Many of the historic coats-of-arms in Scotland have the saltire, from time
immemorial the symbol of Saint Andrew, as the principal bearing.
It symbolises the cross on which he suffered martyrdom.*

Catholic and Episcopalian, Presbyterian and Covenanter, all to have embraced it. The badge of the Conservator of Scottish Privileges in the Netherlands, an office dating from the mid 15th century, has attached a small shield bearing the figure of St. Andrew (a somewhat similar badge to that used today by the St. Andrew's Ambulance Association). By the end of the 14th century, the saltire is also making its appearance on Scottish coinage, notably coins issued by David II (1329 – 71) and Robert II (1371 – 90).

It was during the reign of James IV (1488 – 1515) that the Scottish navy was at its greatest strength. The greatest warship of its

Built for King James IV in 1511 the Great Michael was, in its day,
the largest warship in the World. It was said to have been over 240 feet long
with 35 big guns, 300 small artillery, 120 gunners and 1,000 soldiers.
The model above is at the Royal Scottish Museum.

day, the 'Great Michael', was the dreadnought of its time and it is recorded that no less a sum than £72.7s.6d. was expended on her flag, the "mayn standert", in 1513. This flag appears to have had a St. Andrew's Cross on a blue ground at the head, and a fly of red and yellow – the king's livery colours – on which the royal badges of of the red lion and white unicorn appeared.

During the reign of James IV, the great Scottish admiral, Sir Andrew Barton, fell while fighting the English aboard his ship the 'Lion'. As he died he exhorted his men to "stand fast by the Cross of St. Andrew." His heroic last stand was immortalised in the famous old ballad.

"Fight on, my men," Sir Andrew says,
"A little I'm hurt, but yet not slain;
I'll but lie down and bleed a while,
And then I'll rise and fight again.

"Fight on, my men,"Sir Andrew says,
"And never flinch before the foe,
And stand fast by St. Andrew's Cross,
Until you hear my whistle blow."

They never heard the whistle blow,
Which made their hearts wax sore adread,
Then Horsly said, "Aboard my Lord,
For well I wot Sir Andrew's dead."

Scottish ship flying the national flag, from a carved stone panel at Newhaven, date 1588.

Quite frequently, mediaeval cartographers embellished their maps with shields or banners of royal or national arms. In the Portugese Cantino map of 1502, preserved at Modena, Scotland bears a shield charged with a St. Andrew's Cross.

In 1498, during the reign of James IV, Pedro de Ayala visited Scotland as the ambassador of the King of Spain. In his account of the visit he makes mention of the national flag. *"Scotland has succoured most of her neighbours. With respect to France and Flanders this is notorious. The Dukes of Burgundy wear the tan of St. Andrew [a corruption of the heraldic term 'tau' for a cross] in memory of the succour which Scotland sent to Duke [not named in the original document]. St. Andrew is the patron Saint of Scotland."*

In the arms of the border town of Hawick is a flag bearing the St. Andrew's Cross with the date 1514. The flag commemorates the defeat of English insurgents by the burgesses of Hawick at Hornshole in that year. It is discussed by the Marquis of Bute in his 'Arms of Royal and Parliamentary Burghs': "It is simply the national flag and the date is inscribed upon it in the same way as is often done in the colours of regiments." He also alludes to the two flags which do duty as supporters, the dexter charged with a saltire, the sinister, another of the same, surmounted by an open crown. "The first is, of course, the national flag, the second, a variant of that flag used by the kings." There is one in the painted decoration of the time of Charles I, on the ceiling of the Chapel Royal of Falkland Palace, and another in the picture representing James VI as a child praying beside the tomb of his father in the Abbey Church of Holyrood, where the flag is represented as hanging down from the wall. It is a variation of the national flag as used by the monarch.

An English traveller in Scotland in 1558 writes of the apostle being the patron Saint of Scotland, and adds that the "Scots used to carry a St. Andrew's Cross to war." This is confirmed by the apparently disapproving observations of Bishop Hooper who wrote in 1549 that, "The English called upon St. George, the French St. Denis, and the Scots St. Andrew, as though their private Gods and singular patrons could give the victory and upper hand in the field, or St. George favour him that St. Andrew hateth." A 15th century stained glass window in

Doddiscombsleigh, Devon, has figures of St. George, St. Andrew and St. Patrick, indicating that by that time the three were associated as patron saints of their respective territories throughout Britain.

By the beginning of the 16th century, the flag is assuming the role of essential decoration and embellishment far removed from its original purely military usage. In the accounts of the Lord High Treasurer for 1512 there is recorded a payment for a roll of blue "say" [woolen cloth] for the banner of a ship "with Sanct Androis Cors in the Myddis." Just before the Battle of Flodden – the following year – there was a great rush to make ready the flags. The Lord High Treasurer's accounts for August of that year detail the work:

Item for four ellis rede taffeteis to make Sanct
Adrowis and Sanct Margarettis Baneris £4 0 0

Item for four ellis rede taffeteis to be the King's Baner . . £4 0 0

Item for 14 unce of sewing silk to be frenzies to
the Baneris and Standartis £3 0 0

Item three ellis taffeteis to be the King's Standert £3 0 0

Item to ane woman that maid the frenzies to the
Baner and Standertis. 40/-

Item for making of then in haste. 4/-

Item to ane man to byde on the standartis to bring
thaim with him in haist that nycht that the King's Grace
departed furth of Edinburgh 10/-

It is fascinating to note that little changes in human behaviour over the years: a healthy excess for the rush job obviously put in hand at the last moment. The "baners" referred to would have been rectangular or square flags bearing the arms of the owner. In the case of James IV, the banner would have consisted of the red rampant lion and double tressure flory counterflory of the Scottish kings. The standard was a long tapering flag on which were emblazoned the badges and motto of the owner. In the place of honour – the section next to the pole – the national device was inserted: in England, the Cross of St. George and, in Scotland, the Cross of St. Andrew.

The importance of the use of the national devices can be understood when you imagine the confused maelstrom that must have constituted mediaeval battle. In the general melee the charges on the standards must have been difficult to distinguish but the national emblem would have been clear to all, indicating to friend and foe alike who were the leaders. The crosses of St. Andrew and St. George were so strikingly dissimilar in colour and form as to be easily recognisable in the heat of battle.

The standard was normally split at the end and varied in size according to the rank of the person entitled to it – that of a king was eight yards long while that of a knight was but four. Several Scottish standards have been preserved to this day. One of the more interesting is the Douglas Standard, kept in the National Museum of Antiquities in Edinburgh. It is said to have been carried by Archibald Douglas, son of the second Earl of Douglas, at the Battle of Otterburn in 1388. The flag is of sage green silk and has the St. Andrew's Cross at the hoist, with a red heart between the lower extremities and another at the top of the sinister side. Possibly there was a third at the dexter side also, but this part of the flag has been torn away. A fine lion passant, a mullet, a tau cross, and the motto "James Areyre" appear on the fly of the flag. The devices have been painted onto the flag, and the saltire is now a greyish black, probably due to the oxidisation of the white pigment originally used. The actual date it was made is the subject of some speculation but its importance is not in dispute. In 1918 the then Lord Lyon, Sir J Balfour Paul, opined that it was "one of the most interesting relics to have come down to us from the days of chivalry."

Standard of the Earl of Douglas,

Standard of Keith, the Earl Marischal.

The Marchmont Standard is believed to date from around the beginning of the 16th century. It was the standard of the Warden of the Marches. It bears next to the pole the Scottish saltire which, however, is couped, badge fashion, in that it does not extend to the edge of the flag. The flag is charged with a lion rampant which is also found on the shield of the Homes, the motto "Keyp Reuill", and two popinjays or parrots (also found in the Home arms). The saltire must also have appeared on the Keith Standard carried at Flodden but it unfortunately has been torn just at the point where the saltire would have been.

Another early standard bearing the saltire is that known as the Blue Blanket of Edinburgh, said to have been given to the Incorporated trades of the capital by James III and his Queen, Margaret, the latter of whom, according to tradition, embroidered it with her own fair hands. The flag is of blue cloth and has a white saltire in the upper corner, with a crown and thistle between the upper and lower arms respectively.

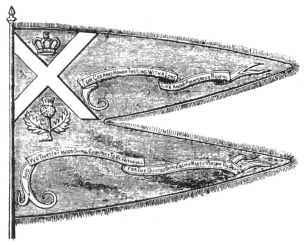

The "Blue Blanket" of the Trades of Edinburgh

14

Another interesting trades flag is that of the seven Incorporated Trades of Stirling, now held by the Smith Institute there. The flag is of a light blue colour and has seven vertical white stripes indicating the number of the Trades. Over all is borne the white saltire of Scotland. This flag is supposed, according to popular legend, to have been the gift of Mary Queen of Scots to the tradesmen of the Royal Burgh and to have been made by the women of her court. Other experts think that it may rather have been the gift of her mother, Mary of Guise, who was more closely associated with Stirling.

A correspondent of Sir Walter Scott, one Joseph Train, has left an interesting description of some ancient furniture then to be found at Threave Castle in Galloway. On an old "buistie", or bedstead, which Train asserts had belonged to William, the Black Earl of Douglas who was assassinated in Stirling Castle in 1452, there were carved a number of soldiers, both horsemen and footmen. "The first foot-soldier bears the 'handsynie' [standard] to which is attached a forked streamer with a saltire or St. Andrew's Cross. The national banner is supported by a sturdy billman."

The standards borne at the funerals of Mary Queen of Scots and of her son James VI also had the saltire in the place of honour. A similar standard was borne at the funeral of Oliver Cromwell. A contemporary observer reported, "At the head, on the left side, stands the great standard of Scotland, viz. in the head Azure, a saltire Argent; in the trayle, a lion sejant on a crown Gules, with a sceptre in his dexter paw Gold, and a sword in the other proper, and this motto: – In My Defence God Me Defend. In the middle, on the left hand, stands the great baner of Scotland, viz. Azure, a saltire Argent."

With the approach of the Reformation, religious interest in saints and their banners goes into some decline. The saltire, however, is by now such an established and popular feature of life in Scotland that there is no danger of it being replaced as the people's national flag, although from time to time there was pressure for the use of the royal standard, which showed the unicorn as the dexter supporter upholding the St. Andrew flag, while on the sinister the lion upholds that of St. George. The Scrymgeour family, who are the Hereditary Standard

Bearers of Scotland, having held that office from early times, have, as supporters of their arms, two stag hounds which hold the Royal banner and national banner respectively, as in the Royal Arms.

During the troubled post-Reformation period the St. Andrew flag came into increasingly popular use. Preserved at Holyrood Palace there is a coloured drawing of the confrontation between the Confederate Lords and Queen Mary at Carbery Hill. Clearly visible are the armorial banners of the lords, the Royal banner and no less than four large flags bearing the saltire. At the siege of of Edinburgh 1572 – 3, when the castle was held for Queen Mary under the attack by the Regent Morton, both parties of the Scots used the national flag and the English used the Cross of St. George.

Around this time, the national flag became widely recognised as that of Scottish shipping at a time of burgeoning international trade. A number of royal burghs situated on the sea coast already had a ship as part of their coat of arms, and many beflagged the ship with the St. Andrew's Cross. Kirkwall, Stranraer, Port Glasgow, Wigtown, Greenock and North Berwick are among those showing the flag in this way.

Many burgh crosses were decorated with the saltire, often on a shield borne by a unicorn. One of the most ancient and interesting is that at Inverkeithing in Fife. It dates from the 14th century. On the capital there are four shields: one and two are the royal shield for King Robert II; three that for Queen Annabella; and number four for Douglas. It is believed that the cross dates from 1398, the date of the marriage of King Robert's son, David, to the daughter of the Earl of Douglas. The ancient cross is topped by a unicorn bearing a saltire. The cross of Inverness has a plain capital with a square tablet bearing the St. Andrew Cross. According to a drawing in the book 'Scottish Market Crosses', the ancient cross of Perth used to bear a staff to which a metal flag bearing the saltire was attached.

After King James VI of Scotland, and James I of England, ascended the throne there arose some confusion as to what flags should be shown and a proclamation was perforce issued on April 12 1606 "declaring what flags South and North Britons should bear at sea." This proclamation is interesting because it contains the first recorded reference to the British national flag, commonly known as the Union Jack. "All our subjects in this our isle and kingdom of Great Britain and the members thereof, shall bear in their main top the red cross commonly called St. George's Cross and the white cross commonly called St. Andrew's Cross joined together according to a form made by our heralds and sent by us to our Admiral to be published to our said subjects." But, in addition to this flag, the subjects of South Britain were to fly on their fore-top "the red cross only as they were wont" and, similarly, the Scots in their fore-tops "the white cross only as they were accustomed." At Hampton Court there is a picture showing a 17th century Scottish warship: it is flying a blue flag with a white saltire in the canton.

The Union Flag, unlike the two flags out of which it was made, seems to have been intended at first for use only at sea. In fact, the very name – Union Jack – is derived from its use on the jack staff of the ship. The English seem to have taken quite kindly to the use of the flag but not so much the Scots. A letter was sent from Edinburgh addressed to their "most sacred soveraigne" in which they complained bitterly that the new flag was *very prejudiciall to the fredome and dignitie of this estate, and will gife occasion of reprotche to this natioun quhairevir the said flage sal happin to be worne beyond sea, becaus, as your Majestie may persave, the Scottis Croce called Sanct Androis Croce is twyse divydit and Inglishe Croce callet Sanct George haldin haill and drawne through the Scottish Croce, whiche is thairby obscurit, and no takin nor merk to be seene of the Scottis Armes. This will breid some heit and miscontentment betwixt your Majesties subjectis, and it is to be feirit that some inconvenientis sall fall oute betwixt theme, for oure sea fairing men cannot be inducit to ressave that flag as it is set doun. They haif drawne two new drauchtis and patronis as most indifferent [fair] for boith kingdomes whiche they presented to the Counsell and craved our approbatioun of the same, but we haif reserved that to your Magesties Princelie determination, as more particularlie the Erll of Mar, who was present and hard their complaynt, and to whom we haif remittit the discourse and delyverie of that matter, will inform your Majesty, and latt your Heyness see the errour of the first patrone and indifferencie of the two new drauchtis."*

Unfortunately no copy remains of these suggested new designs and it is suspected that they perished in the same fire that destroyed the original pattern of the Union Flag made by the English Heralds. In any case, King James VI does not appear to have taken any notice of the complaint but, that notwithstanding, the Scots went ahead and a Union flag of quite another form was put into use in Scotland. On this flag, the cross of St. Andrew was laid over that of St. George. It seems to have been used officially: when King James visited Dumfries in 1618 he was presented with an address in which he was hailed as the king under "whose scepter the whyte and reid croces are so proportionablie interlaced." The Scottish cross had the place of honour as it did in Slezer's engraving of 1693 for 'Theatrium Scotiae' in which it is shown flying from the flagstaff of Edinburgh Castle (Slezer was Captain of Artillery and Surveyor-General of Stores and Magazines in Scotland).

**Flown on Edinburgh Castle about 1693,
showing the sctotish Saltire over the English cross,
from Slezer' engraving**

In the early 17th century King Charles I granted ensigns armorial to the colony of Nova Scotia. This part of Canada has always been most closely associated with Scotland – indeed, today, there are more Nova Scotians speaking the Gaelic than Scots in Scotland who have the language. In 1621 a charter was granted to Sir William Alexander for the colonisation of the area lying between New England and Newfoundland. The ensigns were founded on the Scottish national flag and consisted of a silver shield with a blue St. Andrew's Cross on it. Twelve years later, Sir William Alexander was created Earl of Stirling and Viscount of Canada and he was allowed to put the arms of the colony on the first quarter of his own shield.

The 17th century was a troubled time in Scotland. In 1639 the Scots, in defence of their liberties, took up arms against King Charles and it is recorded that "everie companie had flying at the Captain's tent doore a brave new colour stamped with the Scottish Armes this ditton 'For Christ's Croun and Covenant.'" Alexander Leslie, who was created Earl of Leven two years later, took as supporters for his arms "two ensigns in uniform each holding in his exterior hand a banner gules with a canton azure charged with a silver argent."

At the battles of Preston (1648) and Dunbar (1650) the Scots armies this time suffered heavily at the hands of Cromwell and a large number of their colours fell into the hands of the English. All the actual flags themselves have perished but, thanks to the diligence of 'The historiographer of His Highnesse Oliver Cromwell', the British Museum has a collection of no less than 223 drawings of them. Of the Scottish standards that were taken, some did come back to Scotland: the flag of Colonel Scott's Regiment of Horse carried at Dunbar is still preserved in Edinburgh. It is made of silk and measures five foot three inches in length and four foot four inches in depth. It bears the white saltire on a blue field. There is another flag of this time extant: that which Stewart of Garscube carried with him on the ill-fated expedition to Worcester in 1651. This flag also bears the white saltire but on a field quartered blue and pink. Of the 197 more or less complete drawings made by the Historiographer, no fewer than 150 show the saltire in one form or another. Many are simple saltires, others have the national flag in a corner of a larger flag. Fifteen have the white saltire on a black background and red, green and, even, golden fields are to be found. These different coloured fields were probably to indicate troop and company colours and, of course, many were home made productions. Some of the flags bear the badges of the leaders, a few have their mottoes. The Scottish Parliament of 1650 had ordered that upon the "haill culloris and standards there be 'Covenant for Religion King and Kingdomes'" and on flags from both Preston and Dunbar these words frequently appear.

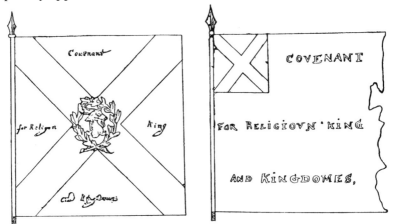

Scottish colours captured by Cromwell at Preston, 1648.

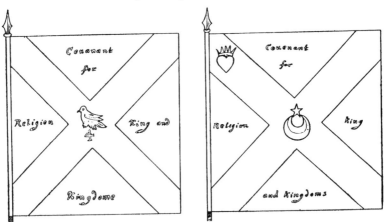

Scottish colours captured by Cromwell at Dunbar, 1650.

The banner of St. Andrew was the flag Scotsmen took abroad with them over the centuries when they went to fight in foreign wars, either as allies or as mercenaries. In Sir Walter Scott's 'Quentin Durward' the uniform of the Scottish archers in France included a loose surcoat or cassock of rich velvet, open at the sides like that of a herald to facilitate movement, and it bore a large white St. Andrew's Cross of embroidered silver bisecting it before and behind. The Douglas Regiment in France carried with it the old blue banner. The Green Brigade, which was originally formed by Hepburn for service with Gustavus Adolphus, and which later joined with its Scottish comrades in France to form the Regiment d'Hebron, later became known as the Royal Regiment of Foot, the first Royal Scots. Its uniform was originally green with standards in that colour, on which there was the saltire in the canton. Two flags of this type were carved on the monument erected to William, Duke of Hamilton, in Bothwell Parish Church (1694).

With the coming to power of Oliver Cromwell, an edict was issued which commanded "all the people of Scotland and of the Isles of Orkney and Zetland and of all the Dominions and Territories belonging unto Scotland are and shall be and are hereby incorporated into, constituted, established, declared and confirmed one Commonwealth with England ... and be it further ordained ... that the Arms of Scotland, viz. a cross commonly called the St. Andrew's Cross, be received into and borne from henceforth in the Arms of this Commonwealth ... and that all Public Seals, Seals of Office and Seals of Bodies Civil or Corporate in Scotland which heretofore carried the Arms of the King of Scotland shall from henceforth instead thereof carry the Arms of this Commonwealth." This order was sent from London on April 22 1654 and published throughout Scotland.

For some time the National Flag was used in a new form: a flag quartered like the Royal Banner with, in its first and fourth quarters, the St. George's Cross and, in its second and third, the St. Andrew's Cross. The banner of Cromwell, Lord Protector of the Commonwealth, was similar but it bore, in addition, a shield with his personal arms and the third quarter contained the Irish harp instead of the St. Andrew's Cross.

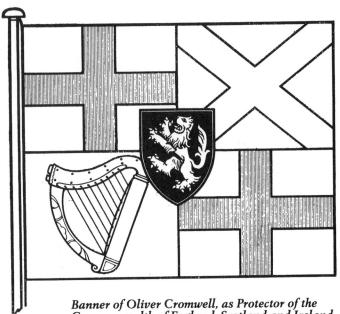

Banner of Oliver Cromwell, as Protector of the
Commonwealth of England, Scotland and Ireland.

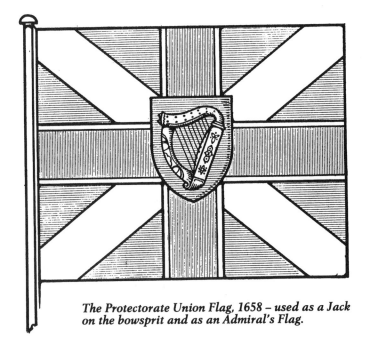

The Protectorate Union Flag, 1658 – used as a Jack
on the bowsprit and as an Admiral's Flag.

The Great Seal during the Commonwealth followed the Scottish design rather than the English. It showed on the obverse Cromwell on horseback, and on the reverse a shield bearing the crosses of St. George in the first and fourth quarters, the Cross of St. Andrew in the second, and the harp of Ireland in the third. Over all, there was a small shield bearing Cromwell's own arms. It was soon found inconvenient to send Scottish charters to England and so a Great Seal was made for Scotland in 1656. It bore the effigy of the Protector on the obverse, and on the reverse a shield bearing St. Andrew's Cross, surmounted by Cromwell's own arms in an inescutcheon. Naval medals, issued in 1653, were similarly designed and bore three united shields, with St. Andrew's Cross, St. George's Cross and the Irish harp.

During this period, as one might expect, the royal emblems were discarded and, indeed, the national ones came into even wider usage – despite the fact that, to the stalwart Puritans of those days, the use of crosses was to a large extent anathema. This was despite the imprecation in the 'Larger Catechism' that "all superstitious devices, whether invented and taken up of ourselves, or received by tradition from others, though under the title of antiquity, custom, devotion, good intent, or any other pretence whatsoever" were to be regarded as violations of the second commandment.

With the return of the King to the throne in 1660 the old regiment of the Scots Guards was revived and by January 1661 a company had taken up duty at Edinburgh Castle. By September 1662, six companies had been raised and later that month they were presented with new colours. These colours were red, with the white St. Andrew's Cross on the blue canton. In the centre was the thistle surmounted by a crown and encircled with the motto "Nemo me impune lacessit." A book published in 1682 – "The Present State of Scotland" – has an interesting frontispiece depicting Mars crowning the Scottish Army with victory. Beside the leader is a standard bearer holding aloft the blue and white flag of Scotland. The design indicates that at this time the army as well as the Covenanters was using the national flag. A contemporary picture also shows the St. Andrew's Cross flying from the flagstaff at Edinburgh Castle.

Similarly, an observer of the military review by Charles II at Putney Heath in 1684 observes that the Royal Regiment of Foot, commanded by the Earl of Dumbarton, "flyes a St. Andrew's cross with a thistle and crown, circumscribed in the centre Nemo me impune lacessit."

During the reigns of Charles II and James VII the Covenanters of Scotland rose up to defend their liberties and took as their banner the old blue and white flag of Scotland. A number of flags of this period survive. The flag carried by the Covenanters of Avondale at Drumclog and Bothwell has the St. Andrew's Cross on a canton with the inscription, "Avondale For Religion, Covenants and Kingdomes". Another, carried by the Ayrshire Covenanters, bears the St. Andrew's Cross of white on a blue ground next to the staff with the motto on the fly, "Pro Religione et Libertate." The national flag became so closely associated with the Covenanting movement that right up until the beginning of this century it was known in many parts of Scotland as the Blue Banner of the Covenant and the purview of "the Hillmen." Yet, in actual fact, it conjoined the Scots rather than divided them.

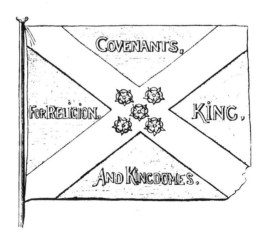

Flag of the Covenanters, said to have been carried at the Battle of Bothwell Brig, 1679, and again in 1745 by a body of volunteers in Edinburgh.

Andrew Ross, in 'Old Scottish Regimental Colours' avers that, *"The banner of St. Andrew with its spotless cross was alike the emblem of Queen Mary and King James, of Jacobite and Covenanter. His national flag the Scotsman carried abroad, and whether serving as a good Catholic in the ranks of the Most Christian King, or as a stout Protestant in the armies of the Netherlands, he preferred to fight under its folds."* The Scot who fights abroad is a potent image throughout Europe: *"none in Europe sent forth more or bolder adventurers"* as Scott put it. This is a tradition which has continued right up to the end of the 20th century. As recently as the beginning of 1992, Scots mercenary soldiers fighting in the frontline in Croatia were to be seen with the cross of St. Andrew sewn onto the sleeves or shoulders of their uniforms.

During the reign of James VII the order of the Thistle was revived and eight knights were invested with the insignia of the Order. In earlier days, the Order had often been known as the Order of St. Andrew and this was reflected in the insignia: the Star consists of a saltire of silver with rays emanating between the arms and in the centre is a thistle surmounted by the motto of the Order. The new ribbon was green – a departure from the original colours of blue and white which reflected those of the national flag.

In 1672, by Act of Parliament, the legal jurisidiction over the display of flags in Scotland came within the sole discretion of a Scottish authority, the Lord Lyon King of Arms. He remains to this day supreme in heraldic matters throughout Scotland – supreme over any other court or, even, government body or department operating in Scotland. In recent years, even the feared department of Her Majesty's Customs and Excise were obliged by him to remove the coat of arms from above the door of their Edinburgh headquarters .

The ascendancy of William of Orange brought to an end the troubles in Scotland and within two decades the Union of England and Scotland had taken place. During William's reign there was an interesting byway of Scottish history not without relevance to the flag. The great Scottish Colonisation Scheme – more popularly known as the ill-fated Darien Scheme – was launched. The Scheme was to be carried on by the "Company of Scotland trading to Africa and the Indies." The company registered its arms in 1696 and they consisted of the Scottish Shield with a ship under sail flying the Scottish flag between the upper arms of the Cross, a Peruvian sheep in base, with a camel and an elephant in the dexter and sinister flanks respectively. The expedition itself consisted of three armed ships: the 'St. Andrew', the 'Caledonia' and the 'Unicorn', along with two smaller vessels, the 'Dolphin' and the 'Endeavour'. They sailed from Leith on July 17 1698 and arrived at the Isthmus of Panama the following November. Here the putative colonists took possession of some unoccupied territory, built a fortress which they called Fort St. Andrew and founded a colony which they optimistically named New Caledonia. The flag of the new – and shortlived – colony was similar to that of the trading company but had, in addition, a red escutcheon charged with a crowned thistle head. The whole venture ended in disaster in the face of disease and poor planning.

This was, nevertheless, a time marked by the beginning of a great era of Scottish commercial prosperity and many enduring enterprises date from it. Institutions like the Bank of Scotland and the Edinburgh Merchant Company were founded. It is a measure of the perceived importance of the saltire that it was incorporated in the arms of both. To this day, the arms of the Bank of Scotland remain a saltire of white on a blue field (or blue where is no field) with four besants (representing gold coins) between the arms of the cross. The shield of the Edinburgh Merchant Company (1693) is charged with a ship "flagged of Scotland."

The College of Surgeons, Edinburgh, who entered their arms a couple of decades earlier, have the national arms surmounted by a crowned thistle in the canton of their shield. Other great societies incorporated in the 18th century such as the Society of Antiquaries of Scotland and the Writers to His Majesty's Signet have the saltire argent on azure as the main part of their arms. The arms of the University of Edinburgh, founded in 1582, have a saltire azure as the principal charge on a silver field. The seal of the Court of the Lord Lyon has the saltire in chief and it also was to form the principal charge in the arms of Trinity College, Glenalmond, and the Royal Technical College, Glasgow.

Society of Antiquaries of Scotland

Bank of Scotland ∴ ❖

Writers to H.M.Signet

Glasgow Royal ❖
❖ Technical College

The Scottish Cross forms the principal bearing in the arms of many public bodies in Scotland. The four examples above are given from Lyon Register.

27

The saltire has, through history, been adopted by many of the great Scottish regiments. The Royal Scots put St. Andrew with his cross on their buckles and the star of the Order of the Thistle on their cap badges – this already incorporating a St. Andrew's Cross with rays emanating between the arms. The King's Own Scottish Borderers also wore the saltire on their cap badge and the Black Watch adopted it on both their collar and cap badges. The Highland Light Infantry wore the bugle – a distinguishing sign of light infantry regiments – on a broad chequered saltire. The Gordon Highlanders' badge consisted of a stag's head rising from a ducal coronet; all this surrounded by a thistle wreath and the whole resting on a St. Andrew's Cross. The Queen's Own Cameron Highlanders took as their cap badge the figure of St. Andrew with his cross, surrounded by a wreath of thistles, while the renowned territorial regiment, the London Scottish, adopted a lion rampant on a saltire within a thistle wreath. Alas, today, so many of these proud regiments with their great historical traditions are now but memories. But that ancient and enduring body of men, The Royal Company of Archers, which still provides the royal bodyguard in Scotland, albeit now picturesquely ceremonial, carry on their colours the figure of St. Andrew on his cross.

With the Union of 1707, Scotland and England were joined together and both parties lost much in the way of identity and individual institutions. One such consequence was that each nation ceased to have a separate national flag. This important and contentious matter was, accordingly, dealt with in the First Article of Union:

That the two kingdoms of Scotland and England shall, upon the first day of May next ensuing the date hereof, and for ever after, be united into one kingdom by the name of Great Britain, and that the ensigns armorial of the said United Kingdom be such as Her majesty shall appoint, and the crosses of St. George and St. Andrew be conjoined in such a manner as Her majesty shall think fit, and used in all flags, banners, standards, and ensigns, both at sea and land.

The inference is clear. The "ensigns armorial" [Royal Arms] are recognised as being entirely under the control of Queen Anne. But the national flag, which is to consist of the separate national crosses, can be

Royal Thistle ∴ ∴ Badge

The Queen's badge for Scotland, dates from reign of King James III.

Royal Saltire ❖ ❖ Badge

Silver Cross enfiled by an open crown gold.

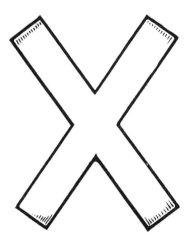

Saltire Badge : ❖ of the Scots

The silver cross of Saint Andrew was and is the distinguising mark of the Scottish people.

Thistle Floral : ❖ Badge

Used to distinguish an owner's property and worn by his servants and retainers.

conjoined only by the Queen as she might see fit. In fact, Her Majesty duly saw fit to make the Scottish flag the ground of the new one, placing thereon that of St. George and this continued to the Union Flag – commonly, and erroneously, termed the Union Jack – until 1801 when the so-called cross of St. Patrick was added. This last was, in fact, really the red saltire of the Fitzgerald arms and without the deeper traditional significance of the crosses it joined.

The new arrangements were not generally welcomed – neither in Scotland nor in England. The English were given to protest that the white field of St. George's Cross was obscured by the St. Andrew's blue. The Scots were much energised by the fact that the St. George's Cross was left entire and not only obscured the cross of St. Andrew, but also cut it into pieces. This was construed by many as a deliberate slur on the Scottish nation.

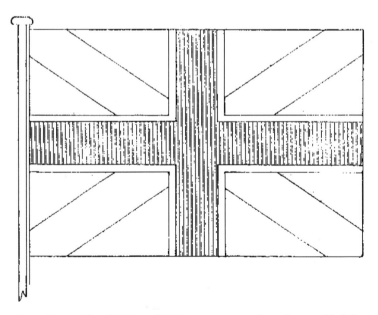

First Union Flag, 1606 and 1707 – appears to have been called the "Britain" or "British Flag". It became the National Flag of Great Britain at the Union in 1707.

To add insult to injury, in spite of the provisions of the Treaty of Union, the predominant partner, i.e. England, continued to use her national flag in the armed services, many regiments carrying the St. George's Cross as a second or regimental colour. It was to be two hundred years before four stands of colours, with the blue banner of Scotland as second colour, were eventually presented to the Highland Light Infantry during the Great War of 1914-18. Thus, it is only in this century that the saltire has made a reappearance on the battlefield, most recently being noted in the Gulf War.

At the Union with Ireland a red saltire was added to the Union Flag and a proclamation was given to this effect on January 1, 1801.

In the Royal Navy the flag of England is predominant – indeed, to a quite unconstitutional degree it might be argued. Only the white ensign consists of a St. George's Cross flag with a small and relatively insignificant Union in the canton. The Royal Navy, of course, is neither English nor Scottish but British and, therefore, its continued use of the banner and pennons of St. George might be regarded as a strange anomaly when the united crosses should, in fact, be used.

It is curious how so often those who should know better persist in flying the Union Flag upside down. Care should always be taken to ensure that the broad white strip is placed so that it is nearest the top of the flag on the side next to the pole. The broad strip with the blue field represents the Scottish part of the flag and, as Scotland is the most ancient kingdom of the three, its white cross has the place of honour. To fly the flag with the red saltire uppermost is to fly it upside down.

Naturally, after the Act of Union, the use of the St. Andrews Cross on its own was not so general. It was, however, used during the rising of 1715. When Lord Kenmure led his retainers from Galloway to fight for the Chevalier Charles the banner he carried was blue with the saltire in gold. These were the Stewart livery colours and explain the apparent departure from the usual silver of the saltire.

One of the few Jacobite flags to survive the 1745 rising was carried at Culloden by the Appin Clan regiment. It was of light blue silk with a yellow saltire. The regiment was officered by Stewarts and comprised a number of Stewarts of Appin. These colours were, accordingly, determined by those of the family.

Colour of the Appin Clan Regiment, 1745.
A yellow Saint Andrew's cross on a blue field

Curiously, during the Jacobite troubles the saltire was also used by some of the volunteer units on the Government side. It is recorded that a company of Edinburgh men carried such a flag in 1745 in support of the Butcher Cumberland.

During the 19th century the national flag largely fell into desuetude but in the early years of the 20th century it came once again into fashion. The Boys' Brigade, the Boy Scouts and some Girl Guide units adopted it and, in 1914, ex-members of the Boys' Brigade formed the 2nd City of Glasgow Battalion of the Highland Light Infantry. On their first review parade in George Square they marched under the King's and Company colours of the 5th Glasgow Company of the Boys' Brigade – most probably the first time that a battalion of the regular army had marched under the Scottish flag for almost 200 years . . .

There is an interesting connection between the national flag of Scotland and that of the United States of America. The original flag of the American Colonies was composed of 13 stripes with the old Union Flag in the corner. After the revolt of the colonies it was resolved in 1777 that the "flag of the United States be 13 stripes alternately red and white, with thirteen stars white in a blue field representing a new constellation." Thus the English part of the Union Flag was taken away and the Scottish colours were left. In 1873 the intention of this was confirmed by the American writer H K W Wilcox: "The blue field was taken from the Covenanters' banner in Scotland, likewise significant of the league and covenant of the United Colonies against oppression, and likewise involving vigilance, perseverance and justice." This view is corroborated by the fact that, during the American Civil War, one of the flags used by the Confederates not only kept the blue and white colours but actually arranged the stars in the form of a St. Andrew's Cross. Many of the leaders not only claimed Scots descent, but also believed Covenanters to be their ancestors.

A less militant but equally spectacular use of the saltire was demonstrated by the controversial Edinburgh character, the Rev. Alan Cameron who died in April 1991. Known, among other things, as 'Edinburgh's bagpiping minister' he parted company with the Church of Scotland in the 1960s and took up the playing of the pipes for the delectation of tourists on the city's Waverley Bridge or at the foot of The Mound. He cut a fine figure in his kilt – his white braces arranged in the form of a saltire across his chest.

The importance of the national flag of Scotland can only be properly appreciated by considering it in a historical perspective. It has played such a central and enduring role throughout Scottish history that it has effectively ensured its own survival. At the end of the 20th century it is not only to be seen flying as a matter of course alongside the Union Flag, but, on anniversaries like Bannockburn day (June 24) and St. Andrew's Day (November 30) it flies alone, a constant reminder of stirring times. The office of the Lord Lyon will advise that it "is the correct flag for all Scots or Scottish corporate bodies to fly to demonstrate their loyalty and their Scottish nationality."

There are, from time to time, hiccups in such widely accepted arrangements. In November 1991 the chief scrutineer of the Lombard RAC International Rally made Scottish drivers replace the saltires on their competition cars with the Union Flag. Displaying an apparent lack of knowledge of British history, he defended his action by saying, "We had to ask the Welsh drivers to put the Union Jack on their cars as well." One canny Scot, however, neatly sidestepped the rules. Louise Aitken-Walker, from Duns, carried the Union Flag on one side of her Ford and the saltire on the other.

But the flag of St. Andrew still flies – every single day of the year – in the East Lothian village of Athelstaneford in commemoration of its timely appearance there all those centuries ago.

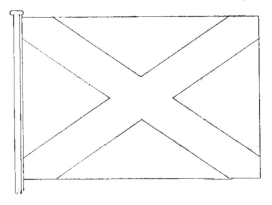

The Scottish National Flag. Banner of Saint Andrew Azure, a saltire argent.

THE SCOTTISH CROSS IN NATIONAL ARMS

NOVA SCOTIA. Silver, a cross of St. Andrew azure, charged with an inescutcheon of the Royal Arms of Scotland. (Lyon Register).

The oldest and grandest of Colonial arms. Granted by King Charles I. These ancient arms were temporarily superseded by arms devised by the English Heralds in 1868; but earlier this century the Government of Nova Scotia decided to resume the use of the old arms.

COMMONWEALTH OF ENGLAND, SCOTLAND AND IRELAND. *1 and 4, Silver, a cross gules (England) ; 2, Azure, a saltire silver (Scotland) ; 3, Azure, a harp gold stringed silver (Ireland). On an inescutcheon sable a lion rampant silver (Cromwell).*

These arms formed Cromwell's banner as Protector. The Protectorate Union Flag was like that of King James VI. and I., but with the addition of the Harp of Ireland on an inescutcheon.

CROMWELL'S SCOTTISH ARMS. *Azure, a saltire silver, on a inescutcheon sable a lion rampant silver.*

The arms for Scotland of Protector Cromwell. The National Flag of Scotland continued without the inescutcheon of Cromwell's personal arms.

COLONY OF CALEDONIA. *Azure, a saltire silver between a ship under sail flagged of Scotland in chief proper, a Peruvian sheep in base a camel on the dexter and an elephant on the sinister proper, the first two loaded and the last bearing a turret silver, over all an inescutcheon gules charged with a thistle head crowned gold.* (Lyon Register, 1698.)

The Scottish Darien, Panama Canal, and Eastern Trading scheme of 1695-1703.

Province of
Nova Scotia

Protector Cromwell's
British Arms

Protector Cromwell's
Scottish Arms

Colony of Caledonia

THE SALTIRE IN ECCLESIASTICAL ARMS

The Saltire or cross of Saint Andrew is of frequent occurrence in ecclesiastical armory. Although a red saltire on a silver field appears as the cross of Saint Patrick in the Badge of the Order of Saint Patrick, 1783, and in the Union Flag, 1801, in so far as the saltire is associated with any saint it is the cross of Saint Andrew alone.

SEE OF EDINBURGH. *Azure, a saltire silver, in chief a mitre of the second garnished gold.*

SEE OF ROCHESTER. *Silver, on a saltire gules an escallop gold.*

The cross of Saint Andrew in these arms alludes to the dedication of Rochester Cathedral to that saint.

SEE OF WELLS. *Azure, a saltire quarterly-quartered gold and silver.*

An interesting and beautiful variation of the cross of Saint Andrew, to whose honour the Cathedral of Wells was dedicated.

SEE OF WAIAPU, NEW ZEALAND. *Azure, a saltire silver, on a canton the arms of the See of Auckland; Azure, three stars, one and two, silver.*

These arms allude to the fact that the See is a district originally settled by Scottish colonists.

The cross of Saint Andrew appears in many other ecclesiastical arms in Britain and beyond.

See of Edinburgh ✣   See of Rochester ✣

See of Wells ✣   ✣ See of Waiapu ✣
✣ New Zealand

ARMORIAL ACHIEVEMENT OF THE KING OF SCOTS

The supporters uphoid the Royal Banner and the National Flag. In the Royal Banner the lion faces the lance, as the lance is deemed to be at the dexter side. To depict the lion with its tail to the lance is an error pointed out by Sir George MacKenzie in his work on Heraldry, 1680.

ARMORIAL ACHIEVEMENT OF THE KING OF BRITAIN

The Royal Arms as officially used in Scotland. The supporters uphold the National Flags of Scotland and England.

SCOTTISH HERALDIC FLAGS

The following material is reproduced from official guidelines by kind permission of the Lord Lyon. All heraldic flags in Scotland come under the legal jurisdiction of the Lord Lyon King of Arms, in terms of the Act of Parliament 1672 cap. 47 and under 30 & 31 Vict. cap. 17. The Lord Lyon's regulations governing the display of heraldic flags in Scotland are broadly as follows. Doubts and questions of exact detail should be referred to the

Court of the Lord Lyon,
HM New Register House,
Edinburgh, EH1 3YT,
Telephone 031-556-7255.

GENERAL

1. SIZE   The size of a flag depends on the site where it is flown, from very small flags for table decoration to enormous flags for the top of a tower. Clear legibility determines the size suitable. Therefore sizes are only given hereafter for special flags, where the sizes are fixed by regulation.

2. PROPORTIONS   The proportions of a flag, the relation of its width to its height, remain constant regardless of its size. Where relevant, these are given hereafter in the form "2:1", i.e. a flag whose width is twice its height.

3. HOIST   The "hoist" is the part of the flag nearest to the pole.

4. FLY   The "fly" is the part of the flag furthest from the pole. In long flags such as Standards, the devices are described in order reading from the hoist to the fly.

5. RESPECTING   All heraldic flags are designed with the convention that the pole is on the left of the flag, from the spectator's point of view. And it is on this convention that the flag and its contents are described. A lion rampant, for example, will face or "respect" the

pole. Heraldic devices are sewn right through the flag's material, so on its reverse side all the devices will be reversed left to right, and the lion will still respect the pole. Lettering on flags such as Standards is the only exception to this rule, otherwise the words would read backwards on the reverse side. Such exceptions have to be of double thickness.

6. MATERIALS Any material suitable to the context and the owner's pocket may be used for flags, from nylon or nylon-and-wool bunting for flags flown out of doors to silk, satin and rich brocades for flags used for internal display. Metallic nylon "Lurex" material gives good and economic results when used for gold and silver.

7. FRINGES Except in a few cases such as Standards, fringes are regarded as mere decoration to be added or omitted at the owner's whim. Where used, they should be either plain and of the same metal (gold or silver) that is predominant in the flag, or they may be of alternate portions of the main colour and the main metal of the flag itself.

8. COLOURS There are no fixed "heraldic colours" for flags. Any red that is clearly "red" and not orange or purple is correct. In general it is found that the brightest possible colours give the best effect The rules of heraldic composition prevent garish results.

9. METALS i.e. Gold and Silver. These occur in almost all heraldic flags, and can be shown either as yellow and white or as metallic gold and silver. Whichever is chosen, its use should be consistent within the flag. Not yellow AND gold.

NATIONAL FLAGS

10. THE UNION FLAG Popularly called "The Union Jack", this is the correct flag for all citizens and corporate bodies of the United Kingdom to fly to demonstrate their loyalty and their nationality. It

is often flown upside down, and the rule is that the broader white diagonals should be uppermost in the hoist, i.e.. next to the pole. Its correct proportions are 2:1.

11. THE SALTIRE   The flag of St. Andrew, the patron Saint of Scotland. Blue with a white or silver diagonal cross reaching to its edges, this is the correct flag for all Scots or Scottish corporate bodies to fly to demonstrate their loyalty and their Scottish nationality. Its proportions are not fixed, but 5:4 is suitable. It is correct both to fly it with or instead of the Union Flag.

12. THE "RAMPANT LION"   This is NOT a national flag and its use by citizens and corporate bodies is entirely wrong. Gold, with a red rampant lion and royal treasure, it is the Scottish Royal banner, and its correct use is restricted to only a few Great Officers who officially represent the Sovereign, including the Secretary of State for Scotland as Keeper of the Great Seal of Scotland, Lord Lieutenants in their Lieutenancies, the Lord High Commissioner to the General Assembly of the Church of Scotland, the Lord Lyon King of Arms, and other lieutenants specially appointed. Its use by other, non-authorised persons is an offence under the Acts 1672 cap.47 and 30 & 31 Vict. cap.17.

BANNERS

13. THE PERSONAL BANNER   This is often wrongly called a "Standard" (see para. 17 below), and is the personal flag of the owner of a coat of arms (an "armiger"). It shows his personal coat of arms granted to him by the Lord Lyon or inherited in right of an ancestor, and protected to him by the Law of Scotland. The coat of arms fills the banner right to its edges, as though it were a rectangular shield. It is quite wrong to use a banner of a plain colour with the owner's arms on a shield in the middle. This would mean that the owner's arms were of that colour with a little inescutcheon in the centre.

Nor should the external "additaments" be shown, i.e. helmet, mantling, crest, motto and supporters. Its purpose is the location and identification of its owner, and it is the visual equivalent of his name. No one else may use it. Flown over his house it denotes that he is there, and as a house flag its proportions are 5:4. The size of a house flag depends on the height of the building and the pole, and it should be large enough to be intelligible at the height at which it is flown.

For personal use, the size and shape varies according to rank, as follows, excluding any fringes:-

The Sovereign	:	60 inches square
Dukes	:	48 inches square
Earls	:	42 inches square
Barons and Feudal Barons:		36 inches square
Other Armigers	:	28 inches wide x 35 inches high

14. CARRYING FLAGS These are personal banners for carrying in processions, either by their owners or their appointed henchmen, for example at Highland Games. They are made of silk or satin or bunting at their owner's choice and may be fringed or not. When so used, there are regulation sizes according to rank, not including any fringes, as follows:-

Peers	:	48 inches wide x 60 inches high
Feudal Barons	:	36 inches wide x 45 inches high
Other Chiefs	:	33 inches wide x 42 inches high
Chieftains	:	30 inches wide x 36 inches high

Other sizes may occasionally be laid down by the Lord Lyon for special occasions.

15. CORPORATION BANNERS   These are the equivalent of personal banners for companies or other corporate bodies, such as Regional or District Councils, which have been granted arms by the Lord Lyon. The flag shows the coat of arms filling its whole rectangular shape, as for personal banners (para. 13). The extent of its usage depends upon the corporate body, whether it is only flown over the headquarters building or at all the company's or corporation's sites. Its use as a car bonnet flag is restricted to the head of the corporate body and when he is acting as such. Its proportions are 5 : 4.

16. PIPE BANNERS   These are banners of personal arms as in para. 13, but cut slanted at the top to fit against the big drone and hang down the piper's back. They are used by most Chiefs and Lairds who have personal pipers, and by the Highland regiments whose company commanders' pipe banners are displayed on the regiment's pipes. The correct usage is for the arms to fill the entire banner to its edges, but some regiments have different customs, such as showing the whole achievement including supporters, or the crest alone. Such traditions are now hallowed by the centuries and are permitted. The pipe-majors of local government or works pipe-bands may display their appropriate pipe-banner of the corporation or company's arms.

SPECIAL HERALDIC FLAGS

17. THE STANDARD   This is a long, narrow tapering flag, granted by the Lord Lyon only to those who have a "following", such as Clan Chiefs, because it is a "Headquarters" flag. It is used to mark the assembly point or headquarters of the Clan or following, and does not necessarily denote the presence of the Standard's owner as his personal banner does. Ancient standards usually showed the national Saltire in the hoist, next to the pole, but nowadays usually show

the owner's personal arms. The remainder of the flag is horizontally divided into two tracts of his "livery colours" for Chiefs of clans or families, three tracts for very major branch-Chieftains, and four for others. Those of peers and barons have the end split into two and rounded. Upon this background are usually displayed the owner's crest and heraldic badges, separated by transverse bands bearing the owner's motto or slogan. The standard is fringed with the alternating livery colours. The height of the standard is not fixed, but it is usually about 4 feet at the pole tapering to about 24 inches at the end. The length of the standard varies according to the rank of its owner, as follows:-

The Sovereign	:	8 yards
Dukes	:	7 yards
Marquises	:	6½ yards
Earls	:	6 yards
Viscounts	:	5½ yards
Lords	:	5 yards
Baronets	:	4½ yards
Knights and Barons	:	4 yards

The standards of non-baronial chiefs, or others who for special reasons get standards, have round unsplit ends.

The height of the flag-pole should take account of the length of the standard when hanging slack.

On rare occasions a uniform length of standard for a decorative display may be laid down by the Lord Lyon.

Where it is desired to display other matter along with the National Flag the Standard is the appropriate form of flag. It should show the Saltire Flag or the Union Jack in the hoist, and the remainder of the flag may contain lettering appropriate to the user's purpose, for example the name of an exhibition or site of a gathering.

18. THE GUIDON This is a similar shape to the Standard, and is one-third shorter than the Standards assigned to Feudal Barons. It is 8 feet long, and is assigned by the Lord Lyon to Lairds who have a following, as for Standards, but are of non-baronial tenure. The Guidon tapers to a round, unsplit end at the fly, has a fringe of the livery colours, and has a background of the livery colours of its owner's arms. The owner's Crest or Badge (formerly his arms without supporters) are shown in the hoist, with his motto or slogan in the fly.

19. THE PENNON This is similar to the Guidon but half its length, i.e. 4 feet. It is assigned to armigers in very rare cases and circumstances nowadays.

20. THE PINSEL This is the flag denoting a person to whom a Clan Chief has delegated his authority for a particular occasion, such as a Clan Gathering when the Chief himself is absent. In a word, the flag of the Chief's representative. It is triangular in shape, 2 feet high at the hoist and tapering to 4 feet 6 inches in width, with a background of the main livery colour of the Chief's arms. On it is shown the Chief's crest, within a strap of the second livery colour and buckle (gold for full Chiefs), bearing the motto, and outside the strap and buckle a gold circlet (outlined in green if the background is not a contrasting colour to gold) inscribed with the Chief's or baron's title. On top of this circlet is set the owner's coronet of rank or his baronial cap. In the fly is shown the owner's plant badge and a scroll inscribed with his slogan or motto. This flag is allotted only to Chiefs or very special Chieftain-barons for practical use, and only upon the specific authority of the Lord Lyon King of Arms.

THE LAW

21. NATIONAL FLAGS   The Union Flag and/or the Scottish Saltire Flag may be freely flown by any Scot or Scottish Corporate body anywhere in Scotland, to demonstrate their nationality and allegiance. No special permission is required, and either or both may correctly be flown.

22. THE "LION RAMPANT"   The personal banner of the King of Scots may NOT be flown by anyone other than those specifically authorised as variously representing the Sovereign, as set out in para. 12 above. Its use by other non-authorised persons is an offence under the Acts 1672 cap.47 and 30 & 31 Vict. cap. 17. The freedom of use accorded to the Saltire Flag is NOT extended to the Scottish Royal Banner.

23. PERSONAL AND CORPORATE HERALDIC FLAGS   All of these are rigorously protected to their owners by the Laws of Arms in Scotland, and they may be flown by no one else. Transgression of the law is an offence, and the Court of the Lord Lyon includes a Procurator Fiscal whose duty it is to prosecute the offenders.